337500 v.es à la Perpend.re

Long. I

N.º 40

Salseur
B. Bordes
Indrein S.ucc
Arrien
la Rivierre
St Martin de Soulan
Vic
Bierts S.ucc
Rin pregoun
St Paul de
Montoulieu
Cela

Fraumalade
Uchentein
Ayet S.ucc
Alos
St Ernin
Rogale S.uc
Aleu
Massat
Saurat
Amplaun
Mereus

Antrach
Bonac
Sentein le
Sentenac
Vic
ous L.
Bedeilhac
Rabat
Surba
Bonpas
Arnave

DEP.T DE L.A R R I E G.

SEIX
Bemajour R.
Erce
COMTÉ
Gourbit S.uc
Niaux
la Pege
Larnat
Bouau
Ornalac

LANGUEDOC
Aleth R.
Suc
Illier
Jun
Caz

Trein d'Ustou
Aulus
Sentenac
Saleus
Vied essos
Surba
Siglos
Larb

St Lizier d'Ustou
Ollier S.uc
Gen.
Signer
 Aston

Conflens
Gouther

Verdehac
Signer R.
DE

Aston R.

L.
Llaforga R.
Rialp R.
Horto

Jucle

la Courtinada
Camillo
Enbalire R.

Vallée
Ordino
d'Andorre

Apal S.uc
la Massone
Encamp

Andorra la
Vella
Pays Neutre

N.º 178
Enw Colombe
ou Coloma
Enbalire
les
Calder S.uc
R.

Ste Julia
de Loria
Romadrieu

Longitude 1.º

Arcabelle

E.

S.

P.

350000 T.ses à la Perpendiculaire de Paris.

Andorran Memories

PHOTOGRAPHS BY

Valentí Claverol

INTRODUCTION

Miguel Angel Canturrí Montanya

VERNACULAR MEMORIES: LIFE, LABOR, AND LANDSCAPE IN ANDORRA

Ellen Handy

THE SPANISH INSTITUTE
THE VALENTÍ CLAVEROL ARCHIVES

TURTLE POINT PRESS

This book is dedicated to the loving memory of Rosa Sesplugas Claverol,

wife, mother, grandmother, great-grandmother, an inspiration to us all.

She will be missed.

CONTENTS

SPONSOR'S STATEMENT

PATRICK T. SIEWERT

Vice President, Eastman Kodak Company
President, Kodak Professional

Kodak Professional, a division of Eastman Kodak Company, is pleased to sponsor the first exhibition in the United States of the photographic works of Valentí Claverol (1902–2000). Organized in cooperation with The Spanish Institute, this exhibition expresses the memories of an Andorran family through images from the recent history of the country.

This retrospective exhibition of Valentí Claverol's work features some one hundred photographs from the Valentí Claverol Archives and the Claverol family. It explores the vital role that photography has played in the history of a small country in the Pyrenees, where, as early as 1876, Valentí Claverol's father, José, demonstrated a passion for photography that in his son became a lifelong vocation.

Kodak Professional has enjoyed a long history with the Claverol family, dating back to the 1920s, when Valentí Claverol started working with Kodak products in Andorra, and continuing today with his son, Josep.

Kodak Professional salutes The Spanish Institute, and its CEO, Inmaculada de Habsburgo, for organizing and hosting this unique exhibition. As a worldwide supporter of the arts, Kodak Professional firmly believes in the power of photography to enrich lives, remember the past, and preserve memories.

We wish the exhibition a wonderful success.

Kodak Professional

FOREWORD

INMACULADA DE HABSBURGO

President

The Spanish Institute

The Spanish Institute in New York is delighted to present *Andorran Memories*, a retro-spective photographic exhibition of works by the late Andorran photographer Valentí Claverol, dedicated to the memory of Rosa Sesplugas Claverol. The artist's sensitive eye captures special moments in the political and communal life of this medieval principality during the first half of the twentieth century. The stark landscapes, the striking views of Romanesque architecture, and the noble images of the Andorran people in their everyday occupations re-create for the viewer the unique lifestyle that this small region in the Pyrenees preserved well into the 1950s. The images will linger in the mind of the viewer as reference points to times past.

We thank the Claverol family and, in particular, the recently departed artist Valentí for documenting so beautifully the history of his country; his son, Josep, and his wife, Christiane Mailhos, for preserving the photographic archive; and his grandson, David, for bringing this exhibition to New York. We are grateful to Kodak Professional, a division of Eastman Kodak Company, for sponsoring *Andorran Memories*, which will provide valu-able understanding of a vanishing culture.

I also take this opportunity to thank the Board of Directors of The Spanish Institute and its charismatic chairman, Dr. Fernando Aleu; the Cultural and Fine Arts Committee, under the leadership of Dr. Lia Schwarz de Lerner; and the staff of the Institute, particu-larly Paloma Jiménez, Director of Programs, and Xochitl Dorsey, Executive Assistant and Programs Coordinator.

PREFACE

DAVID CLAVEROL MAILHOS

Valentí Claverol's work is dear to me not just because he was my grandfather, but also because it conjures a time and a place that are no more, and this in an age in which we take so much for granted. Andorra today differs considerably from the country that Valentí Claverol recorded for posterity. As UNESCO's director general, Federico Mayor Zaragoza, observed, referring to Valentí Claverol's work: "All countries, whether they are big or small, need a historic memory." My grandfather succeeded in providing Andorra with just that.

Valentí Claverol never set out to make money with his archive of photographs; his aim was to make the country known through his images—documentary photographs, postcards, and so on—and thus encourage foreigners to visit. Luckily, he was in the right place at the right time with his camera, and framed many telling images of the changing country.

The collection of photographs being shown at The Spanish Institute and reproduced in this book is not limited to the Pyrenean principality, however. During his time in Barcelona, Valentí Claverol took pictures of that city and its surroundings, and these images, like those of Andorra, recall a vanished life, simpler and slower-paced.

I was initially apprehensive about introducing my grandfather's work in New York. Organizing an exhibit of photographs of a tiny country few Americans have even heard of seemed a questionable pursuit. A close friend of mine buoyed me: "Persevere," she said; "stick with it. Whatever you do, don't lose faith." I am forever indebted to Maria Cristina Anzola for her faith in me. Likewise I am in debt to my parents, Josep and Christiane Claverol, for their love, support, and patience, and my sister, Alexia, for her love and for always listening. I am grateful to Ariana Neumann for believing in me; and to Lara Anabtawi for living and breathing this project with me. Thanks also to Hussein Damirji, the Archives' unofficial attorney, and to Nurita and Chano Rosales, John and Maria Cristina Heimann, Ruth Baxter, Nina Krauthamer, Karl Katz, Lenny Golay and Ray Sherman, Jeanine Bartel, Elizabeth and Andrew Whitton, Wynne Thomas, and Miguel Angel Canturrí Montanya.

Heartfelt thanks to Charlotte and Alexander Whitton for being part of my life.

And of course, I am indebted to Valentí Claverol, photographer, Andorran, gentleman, for being a constant inspiration, and to my grandmother Rosa Sesplugas; indeed, we are all in her debt, for her love and patience in allowing her husband to disappear in the early hours of the morning, when he knew that the light would be just right to take a photograph.

ACKNOWLEDGMENTS

The Valenti Claverol Archives thanks the following:

Eastman Kodak Company for sponsoring the exhibition, and The Spanish Institute for hosting it;

Maria Victoria Gorbeña, for her friendship and support of the project;

Mrs. Inmaculada de Habsburgo of The Spanish Institute, for her assistance throughout this endeavor;

Paloma Jiménez, for her kind cooperation;

Miguel Angel Canturrí Montanya, for his impressive dedication to the Archives, as friend and attorney;

Mr. and Mrs. José Rosales, for their friendship and encouragement;

Mr. and Mrs. John G. Heimann, for their encouragement and hospitality;

Nina Krauthamer, for her dedication and patience;

Lenny Golay and Ray Sherman, for believing in the exhibition from the outset;

Jonathan Rabinowitz, for the idea to bring the Archives to New York;

and

Wynne Thomas, for advocating the project and being a friend of the Archives and the Claverol family.

VERNACULAR MEMORIES: LIFE, LABOR, AND LANDSCAPE IN ANDORRA

ELLEN HANDY

The photographs collected here belong to one of the most precious genres of the medium: records of ordinary life chronicling a long period of time. Both great events as well as everyday incidents were preserved by Valentí Claverol's camera over many decades. The term "vernacular photography" is often used to describe such work; it connotes quotidian themes, variety, and regional specificity. Early-twentieth-century Andorra was an unassuming nation whose visual record has come to assume an exotic character, since it was so unlike the rest of contemporary Europe. These photographs are beguilingly specific in their reference, yet global in their appeal.

A nation small in acreage may grow to the size of a grand empire in memory, for the past is a country of almost infinite extent. Andorra is just such a nation, and one with an exceptional, expansive photographic legacy. The rich visual record compiled by Valentí Claverol recuperates Andorra's past and preserves it in a continuous present. The role of photography as an incarnation of memory is established in European culture, and today's viewers of photographs are adept at finding familiar elements in visual records of alien experiences. Thus do photographs speak in more than one language, to audiences in more than one land.

Andorra's pleasing anachronism during the 1930s and 1940s, when many of these photographs were made, is that of an all but feudal country that survived into the twentieth century. And Claverol, the unofficial photographer laureate of Andorra, is in effect a nineteenth-century photographer living and working in the twentieth century. His meticulously arranged portraits and formally composed landscapes eschew the ephemerality typical of twentieth-century photography and retain the serene craftsmanship typical of the preceding century, recalling the work of Felice Beato and other masters. Ancient objects and traditional folkways have long exerted a fascination on photographers; the medium has an affinity for the vanishing, the outmoded, the endangered, which it arrests, honors, and preserves.

Claverol's pictures mingle old and new in unexpected ways, depicting scenes in which evidence of twentieth-century life contrasts with older customs. A photograph taken in a town square at Easter 1937 shows a pyramidal array of male musicians in their best suits posing with accordion, saxaphone, and other accoutrements before old masonry and stucco walls, at one with an environment redolent of centuries of tradition. A small child in the foreground who places a finger indecorously in his nose unexpectedly animates the ceremonial gravitas of the image with a spice of informality, while the wrinkles in some of the men's suits suggest the infrequency of their public appearances in such attire. Another photograph depicts the blessing of several automobiles on Saint Christopher's Day 1935, no doubt an instance of tradition changing form with the times while preserving its ancient essence.

Among the most interesting of Claverol's photographs are those depicting forms of labor and emphasizing the lack of machinery, industry, and sophisticated technologies. A photograph from the 1930s of a woman in wooden shoes bearing a heavy yoke and buckets preserves a scene more or less unchanged from the Middle Ages, while a more lyrical image from the 1940s depicts a shepherd with a newborn lamb studying the limpid fall of light over his flock nearby. An old woman posed with a spinning wheel before a window opening upon a mountain in the distance in 1940, and a view of the handsome Romanesque church of Santa Coloma with abundant haystacks lying before it appears much as it must have for centuries. These pictures look as if they could, paradoxically, antedate the invention of photography.

Perched as the country is in the mountains between Spain and France, Andorra's relative inaccessibility helped maintain its autonomy and traditions well into the early years of the twentieth century. This geographical position was important in determining its political and historical circumstances, the very shape of its life and local customs. A striking image of the then new road from Andora to France, blocked by a heavy snowfall in 1936, expresses this well, as does the view of the Radio Andorra building in a tenderly pastoral landscape. A radio station, a road, and a body of photographs are paths that can lead both in and out of an otherwise closed world, or influential voices in dialogue with the wider world.

The timelessness of Claverol's pictures is sometimes shattered by manifestations of war and death. A fraught but measured photograph depicts the reading of a death sentence in the town square of Andorra la Vella in 1943, when a dense gathering rounded the corners of the square and left its center eerily empty. Those at the back of the crowd strain to see the solemn spectacle and others pack themselves onto balconies above. More poignant are the identity photographs of groups of Spanish refugees made from 1936 to 1939, during the Spanish Civil War—men who are variously jaunty, pensive, jovial, tense, and afraid, and women stern in the face of the troubles to come.

Claverol's sensitive, thorough, and earnest document of Andorran life recalls the work of such celebrated photographers as August Sander, Eugène Atget, and Paul Strand. But his endeavor was neither a documentary survey nor a purely personal expression. A genuinely vernacular photographer, engaged with the pictorial needs and desires of his community, Claverol was an integral part of the nation that formed his subject. Not an anthropological observer or outsider, he was, rather, a proud participant in the life he chronicled. Emblematic of this is his reflexively metaphoric photograph of a mysteriously smiling girl holding the outsize key to the parliamentary seat, the Casa de la Vall. This image is itself a key to the enduring and universal value of such indigenous photographic practice: just as the Casa de la Vall is the key to the Andorran nation, photography is the key to the past and to memory, and a child is the key to the future.

INTRODUCTION

MIGUEL ANGEL CANTURRÍ MONTANYA

THE ORIGINS OF A NATION

A tiny country 175 square miles in area (about two and a half times the size of the District of Columbia), nestled in the Pyrenees between Spain and France, Andorra had until the twentieth century been largely untouched by the world outside; its last participation in a "world event" was in the late eighth century, when Charlemagne resisted the Moorish invasion of northeastern Spain. Andorra seemed to ignore major historical and cultural developments affecting the rest of Europe, including the Renaissance and the Age of Discovery, the Enlightenment and the end of absolute monarchy, and the growth of modern nations, to reach our era as a throwback to the Middle Ages.

Now a full-fledged state in the international roster, Andorra was for almost a thousand years a personal lordship, first held by the Spanish bishop of Urgell alone and then, from the late thirteenth century on, shared with the French count of Foix. Feudal links between lords, even between secular lords and ecclesiastics, were not uncommon in medieval Europe. By chance, the two men who shared the lordship of Andorra after the 1278 decree by Pope Martin IV establishing joint rule lived in territories that would later be parts of two different countries—Spain in the case of the bishop, France in the case of the count. If the two lords, or co-princes, as they came to be called, had been on the same side of the Pyrenees, Andorra would have been absorbed into one or the other state, and would not have the curious autonomous position that it has today.

For the bishop of Urgell, the succession relates to the episcopal see, which is some fifteen hundred years old. As for the count of Foix, his rights passed to Henry III of Navarre, who became Henry IV of France, and hence to the French crown and later to the French republic. The president of France is thus an heir to the co-principality of Andorra.

Even into the twentieth century, the relationship between the two lords, and the nature of their rulership, accorded with feudal law. But how to uphold this law, which had disappeared from the rest of Europe centuries before? The joint lordship went against the grain of the separation of powers by now standard in many European governments. The co-princes of Andorra controlled the courts and the police force; they made laws and exercised power over the General Council, the country's parliament. Modernity, the political, social, and ideological changes brought on by the Enlightenment, the Industrial Revolution, and national movements in Europe and beyond, had not reached Andorra, or had done so in a diminished and indirect way, and the existing social structure, the isolated and limited population, and poverty and lack of education prevented them from proliferating.

By the early part of the century, however, time began to catch up with Andorra. Popular suffrage was instituted in 1933, though for men only; women would have to wait until 1970.

In 1993, citizens proposed a written democratic constitution, and the reigning co-princes supported the will of the people. The co-principality became a "constitutional dyarchy," with the Andorran populace fully sovereign.

Andorra now has a modern constitution, yet it is still something of an anomaly among current schemes of government. Here is an independent nation almost hidden between two other, larger independent nations, a co-principality that predates modern law and politics. Nonetheless, Andorra has been recognized internationally. It was the 183rd country to be admitted to the United Nations—and it marches proudly with other nations at the Olympic Games.

AN END TO ISOLATION

Until the First World War, Andorra was virtually cut off from the rest of Europe. There was no road to Spain suitable for cars, and such a road to France was not completed until 1932. The population remained stable at about 3,000; emigration solved the problem of "overpopulation" in this agricultural country. The number of dwellings too remained stable, with little if any new construction. Any tillable land was cultivated, and there was little or no change from centuries past in the types of crops or methods of farming.

Public education was lacking, with no organized schools or libraries, and the illiteracy rate was high. Andorra, poor, self-supporting, forgotten, was even more isolated than other Pyrenees settlements that enjoyed the social and economic benefits of belonging to larger, more important nations.

Andorra lived for a long time, as Fray Luis de Léon put it, "*lejos del mundanal ruido,*" far from the madding crowd, and not quite in Horace's *aurea mediocritas,* or golden mean: life was not golden, and the standard was surely below par.

The *Manual Digest,* a text written in 1748 by an Andorran priest trained in canon law, had advised against establishing access routes to the outside world. If fear of foreigners was behind this admonition, just as important a reason for Andorra's isolation was poverty: lack of funds explains the historical lack of roads. Indeed, Andorrans were thankful for the construction of roads and the subsequent contact with the rest of the world. They expressed their gratitude for the road to Spain, built with Spanish money, by installing the first-ever commemorative plaque in the country. In 1932, it was the members of the General Council, representing the people, who approved the construction of the road to France, which was built by a Franco-Spanish company.

The population of Andorra increased significantly in the twentieth century. In 1948, there were 3,400 Andorrans and 700 foreigners; half a century later, there are about 70,000 inhabitants, a fourth of them citizens. Andorra is a member of the United Nations, the Council of Europe, and the Organization for European Economic Cooperation, and has exchanged ambassadors with many foreign states and signed international treaties. Now this ancient, self-contained land, long closed off from the rest of the world, relishes its contacts, which it pursues by cultivating trade and tourism within its borders.

THE PEOPLE

Endogamy, little wealth, emigration: Andorrans were and are a hardy people, toughened by their landscape and climate, and by necessity. In the past they struggled to wrest food from the soil, subsistence farming and raising sheep and cattle being the chief livelihoods. Natural sources of hot water fostered the development of a cottage weaving industry, and water power also promoted a few iron foundries. In winter, when they could not work the land, men often hired themselves out as laborers in Spain and France.

Andorra's geographic position favored some trade—including the small-scale smuggling of tobacco.

A peasant from Arinsal, skillful at cutting timber, holds a cow collar
and a lamb collar, both of which he fashioned, 1940s.

ABOVE: A villager in clogs makes her way over an unpaved
street to get water from the fountain, 1930s.

OPPOSITE: A woman in front of her spinning wheel, 1940.

TOP: Early in the century, tobacco was a significant cottage industry in Andorra, providing jobs for workers like these cigar makers, c. 1905.

BOTTOM: Bears—which have recently been reintroduced into the Pyrenees—died out because of hunting and development. This, the last one, was hunted in 1942.

ABOVE: A couple in the courtyard of their house; amid a water trough,
a fire, the ever-present tobacco hanging to dry, and a spinning wheel, 1950.

OVERLEAF: At Easter 1937, the singers of the parish of Sant Julià
performed on the main square. Behind them, in the process of being
demolished, are a butcher's shop and the prison. On this occasion,
French gendarmes backed up the native accordionist.

Easter singers, mostly children, in traditional dress, boys and
men with sash and Phrygian cap, 1940. They sang in the streets,
and as the man standing at left demonstrates,
collected poultry and wine for an eventual meal.

Festivities in Andorra la Vella, with people dancing the *contrapàs*.
The Catalan sardana was introduced to Andorra in the 1930s.

THE LAND

The best fields for farming and pasture belonged to a few prosperous families. Others had to make do with mountainside slopes, which they terraced.

Sheep and cattle grazed in high mountain meadows in summer. Stone barns called *bordes* were built to store hay.

Pine and fir trees provided a reserve of timber and—together with birch, oak, and holm oak—firewood. Poplar, ash, and willow were also common.

A glimpse of the Radio Andorra building appears through the trees
in this pastoral scene, Andorra la Vella, 1935.

The parish of Andorra la Vella, 1900.

A view of Santa Coloma and its meadows from the rock of Sant Vicenç. The count of Foix wanted to construct what would be the only military castle in Andorra on this promontory, and the bishop of Urgell opposed him. The *pareatge* of 1288 put an end to the dispute; the castle was built, then dismantled.

27

The parish of Andorra la Vella in the 1970s.

A shepherd carries a newborn lamb
that cannot yet walk, c. 1940.

La Margineda, c. 1940. In the foreground is the enclave
of Sant Jordi, which belonged to a foundation set up by an
American in 1916; the enclave is now the property of the
municipality of Andorra la Vella.

The church at Nagol in the parish of Sant Juliá is set off
by the austere landscape, c. 1940.

Andorra la Vella, c. 1950.

The snow-covered village of La Massana, 1930s.

The Romanesque bridge of San Antoni.
In 1003, Saint Ermengol, bishop of Urgell, co-prince of
Andorra, died after falling from such a bridge
while overseeing its construction.

HOUSES

Village houses, built of stone and clay, and roofed in slate, occupied sunny spots that were unsuitable for cultivation. Often cattle were kept inside houses for their milk.

Scarcity and poverty meant that a family's agricultural holdings would not be divided among several sons; a typical farm produced just enough to support one family. The heir, usually the first-born son, received the land and lived in the house. Other sons might take over other family holdings when they married, while the rest were forced to emigrate, most frequently to Spain or France. New houses were seldom built, as heirs remained in the family house.

Dwellings were maintained as well as possible over the centuries. The homes of more important and prosperous citizens were larger, and were distinguished by whitewashing. Ordinary houses, with their bare stone, blended into the rocky landscape. Many of these age-old dwellings have disappeared, and thus the Claverol Archives are an important reference tool for students of Andorran vernacular architecture.

The mill at Canillo, 1940.

ABOVE: The Casa de la Vall, Andorra la Vella.
Under the eaves are pigeon holes.

OPPOSITE: A public fountain in Andorra la Vella. The Barcelona
newspaper *La Vanguardia* published this image on its front page in 1933.

OVERLEAF: The public washbasin, Andorra la Vella, 1936.

A house backing onto a stable atop another building,
which may have been a church, c. 1930.

Inside a typical Andorran house, 1940.

OPPOSITE: Houses in Andorra la Vella, 1930.

ABOVE: The staircase of this village house was modernized
in the 1950s.

47

Houses in a village in Sant Julià parish, 1930.

Andorra la Vella, with the Casa de la Vall on the far left, 1930.

CHURCHES AND MONUMENTS

Andorra counts several Romanesque churches, built between the eleventh and fourteenth centuries, and some Gothic boundary crosses among its historical monuments. Later churches were simple constructions of no programmatic style.

As the French and Spanish co-princes only visited and did not reside in Andorra, they had no palaces of their own there. The economy—the absence of taxes and public treasury—supported the construction or maintenance of ordinary dwellings and little else.

Valentí Claverol built his house and offices
near this stone cross, *la creu grossa.*

A boundary cross alongside a highway, Andorra la Vella, 1950.
(The boy is Josep Claverol.)

ABOVE: Resting at the side of a footpath in 1950 was a monolith
that later mysteriously disappeared. The image, perhaps of
Saint Christopher, was an addition to an ancient menhir.

OVERLEAF: The Romanesque church at Santa Coloma, c. 1940.
The frescoes within were removed and taken to the
Museum of Romanesque Art in Barcelona.

ABOVE: Sant Miquel de Engolasters, c. 1940.

OPPOSITE: The church at Pal, c. 1940.

GOVERNMENT

The Casa de la Vall in Andorra la Vella, the seat of the General Council and the courts, was the only public building in Andorra until the twentieth century. Apart from its parliamentary and judicial functions, it was used as a school and as a meeting place for public associations. Its only decorative element was a series of Gothic frescoes depicting the Passion of Christ.

Each of the six townships, or parishes, of Andorra (there are now seven) had a communal council, and each sent four representatives to the General Council, or parliament, which met on a number of occasions every year in the Casa de la Vall. There were no permanent civil servants, no national budget, and practically no public spending until after the Second World War.

Justice was effectively in the hands of the French and Spanish co-princes. They and their representatives, the *veguers*, appointed three judges, two for trials and one for appeals.

The most recent application of the death penalty in Andorra was in 1942. When the convicted murderer was executed, the procedure followed was that established in the nineteenth century: The sentence was read on the main square in Andorra la Vella, and a seemingly religious procession, complete with clergy, crucifix, and faithful reciting the rosary, accompanied the condemned man to the cemetery, where he was executed.

Until fairly recently, no street or square in Andorra had an official name. The main square at Andorra la Vella hardly needed one: it was in fact the only square, the central location for all important events in the capital and in the country. The sovereign co-rulers were received on the square when they visited, and public announcements were made there. Business was conducted in shops, banks, and the French and Spanish post offices on the square. Processions, festivals, fairs, dances, and casual meetings of Andorrans took place on the main square. And of course, this is where for decades Valentí Claverol ran his photography shop, and focused on the life of his country.

The door of the Casa de la Vall. The key was kept in a
neighboring house until it was stolen by a tourist.

Men twenty-five and older were given the right to vote in 1933.
Before then, only heads of household could vote.

ABOVE: A chamber in the Casa de la Vall with the court in
session, 1943. The chamber is dominated by portraits of
Pope Pius XII and the two co-princes (on the left is that
of Marshal Pétain, the French co-prince at the time).
At the table are the three judges: the French appeals judge, in
the center, and the two *veguers*, or representatives of the two
co-princes, flanking him.

OVERLEAF: A death sentence is read aloud on the main square
of Andorra la Vella on October 10, 1943. Valentí Claverol's shop,
in the center rear, is closed. One can only imagine the hush.

The General Council chamber, with a clerk sitting at the syndics' table. On
the wall hang the robes worn by the councillors on solemn occasions.

The members of the General Council in 1902.
The men in two-pointed hats are the syndics, who presided
over the Council; the men in tricorns are councillors.
(Photograph by José Claverol)

The Catalan artist Joaquim Mir painting the Casa de la Vall
in 1933 (above); and posing with a young admirer in 1936 (opposite).

OPPOSITE: The home of Radio Andorra, 1930. The building, which was a tobacco-processing factory and then a hotel, was destroyed by fire in the 1990s.

ABOVE LEFT: A copy of the front cover of the *Manual Digest of the Neutral Valleys of Andorra*, which treats of the principality's antiquity, government, and religion, its privileges, preeminences, and prerogatives.
Written "at the request of the General Council by the doctor of law Antoni Fiter i Rossell from the village of Ordino, for the better governance and guidance of its patricians, in the year of our Lord 1748," this constituted the authorized history and public law of Andorra for 250 years.

ABOVE CENTER: Fresco of the Prayer in the Garden of Gethsemane, Casa de la Vall.

ABOVE RIGHT: The coat of arms of Andorra, as it appears over the entrance to the Casa de la Vall: the bishop's miter, the arms of the count of Foix (three vertical red bars on a yellow ground), the arms of Catalonia (four yellow and four red bars), and the arms of the count of Béarn (two cows); and below that the Latin motto "United virtue is stronger." Below this the Latin reads: "Behold: These belong to a neutral valley and are the arms by which nobler kingdoms delight to be protected. If alone, o Andorra, they have blessed other peoples, how much the more will they together bring you golden ages!"

PUBLIC ORDER

The police force, founded in 1931, drew from the most respectable male citizens of the six townships. A national guard, for emergencies and other special needs, consisted of heads of household, each of whom was required to supply his own firearm.

In times of trouble, and when the outside world encroached upon Andorra's peaceful isolation, the co-princes dispatched military or police troops. In 1933, for example, French gendarmes (the Spanish co-prince, the bishop of Urgell, had no troops of his own) were sent in to enforce the co-princes' decision to dissolve parliament and install popular suffrage for men, and to impose order when Spanish workers building a hydroelectric power station threatened to strike.

Gendarmes returned in 1936–1939 to protect Andorra during the Spanish Civil War, and again in 1944 during the Second World War. That same year the Spanish co-prince, bishop of Urgell contributed a force of one hundred men from the Guardia Civil, lent to him by the Spanish government to match the French force that had been sent. With the arrival of these foreigners, Andorrans saw military parades for the first time. The novelty aroused curiosity, calmed some, and worried others.

ABOVE: The arrival of French gendarmes, 1933.

OVERLEAF: Gendarmes and locals on the main square
of Andorra la Vella, 1933.

From their viewing stand, secular and religious authorities
of Andorra observe French gendarmes, 1937.

ABOVE: Gendarmes in the main square
of Andorra la Vella, 1933.

OVERLEAF: Gendarmes taking their leave on a rainy day,
main square of Andorra la Vella, 1939.

75

The syndic general (center, with hands folded),
who presided over the Andorran parliament, with officers of the
Spanish co-prince, bishop of Urgell's Civil Guard,
as they are about to leave Andorra, 1945.

The first Andorran police corps,
in front of the Casa de la Vall, 1931.

Members of the episcopal Civil Guard, Spanish troops
called in by the bishop of Urgell, co-prince of Andorra,
during the Spanish Civil War, 1937.

Negotiations among French gendarmes, Spanish soldiers,
and Andorran police at the Andorran–Spanish frontier, 1939.

Soldiers from Franco's army departing Andorra for Spain, 1939.

Members of the *somaten*, the people's militia, during a strike
at the Andorran electrical company, August 26, 1933.

At the end of the Spanish Civil War, soldiers from Franco's
army arrived at the Andorran border; they were met by a single
Andorran policeman and a pro-Franco sympathizer, 1939.

RELIGION AND EDUCATION

The Church was omnipresent in Andorran life. One of the country's co-rulers, after all, was a bishop, holding ecclesiastical and secular power. Public worship and Christian customs were all-important. The only public holidays were religious feasts; there were no political, civic, or cultural observances, let alone military occasions to commemorate.

The six townships of Andorra provided elementary schooling, but not always. The Church oversaw education to some extent, and in the late nineteenth century Spanish nuns from Seu d'Urgell came to teach, but there was never an established religious order or institution to offer comprehensive formal education. The 1748 *Manual Digest* had advised resistance to such incursions, because religious orders might appropriate precious land in the principality. As a result, clerics from abroad never had the opportunity to impart education or foreign culture.

Bishop Iglesias Navarri visiting San Cerni de Canillo, c. 1940.

TOP: The co-prince of Andorra, Joan Benlloch, bishop of Urgell,
who later became cardinal, with members of the General Council, 1913.

BOTTOM: Bishop Benlloch not only made the first swing with a
pickaxe, and inaugurated public works, but also paid for them,
with Spanish money. Here he breaks ground, 1913.

(Photographs by José Claverol)

Bishop Iglesias Navarri, who was from the county of Pallars in
the Pyrenees, served as a chaplain in Franco's army and attained
the rank of colonel. He was appointed bishop of Urgell in 1942.

RIGHT AND FOLLOWING PAGE: September 8, the feast of Our Lady of Meritxell, is a national holiday, the anniversary of the signing of the *pariatges*. Because the Sanctuary of Meritxell was small, a public mass was held outdoors in 1944. The chapel burned down under mysterious circumstances on September 8, 1972, and a new sanctuary, designed by Ricardo Bofill, was built in 1976. Mass is now celebrated there.

Bishop Iglesias Navarri is received under triumphal arches
covered with box tree branches, 1944. Girls celebrating their
First Communion are among those greeting him.

Students at the school of the Sisters of the Sacred Family, 1950.

Boys kindergarten class, 1950.
(Valentí Claverol's son, Josep, is in the third row, far right.)

TRANSPORTATION

As in many cultures, mules and donkeys were used for carrying loads, and oxen pulled carts and plows. The Spanish co-prince, bishop of Urgell, accustomed to riding in a car in his Spanish cathedral town, rode a mule when he visited Andorra.

The internal road network and paved roads linking Andorra to France and Spain were built only in the first third of the twentieth century. Also during that time, the first modern bridges replaced old Romanesque ones. Once Andorra was linked by road to Spain and France, trade, travel, and tourism naturally increased.

OPPOSITE: In the 1930s, mail was delivered on
foot from Spain and France. In winter this postman—
photographed in 1950 after his retirement—skied his route.

PAGES 98–103: The road from Andorra to France, which was
opened in 1932, was often blocked by snow from autumn through
spring. A passage was cleared with pickaxe and shovel, 1936.

On July 10, Saint Christopher's Day, cars were blessed on the
main square of Andorra la Vella, as here in 1935.

104

Coaches with tourists from France would typically stop
in front of Valentí Claverol's shop, c. 1950.

THE SPANISH CIVIL WAR
AND REFUGEES

Andorra has always maintained a strict neutrality. When war raged in neighboring countries, the principality lay low, allying itself with neither side.

During the Spanish Civil War (1936–1939), Spanish refugees—Nationalist, Republican, uncommitted—came to the safe haven of Andorra. All were welcomed, but in view of the danger if they remained in the country and destabilized it by sheer numbers, French gendarmes were sent in to keep order. In 1939, Franco's victory brought the Nationalist army to the gates of Andorra. Reportedly, they were about to invade the country, but mediation by the Vatican and the Spanish co-prince, bishop of Urgell, halted them at the border.

Refugees passing through Andorra needed photographs for their transit documents. Material was in short supply, but Valentí Claverol was resourceful: he photographed people in groups, then cut the pictures for individual use.

PAGES 107–115: Between 1936 and 1939, Andorra received
refugees from everywhere on the political spectrum.

JOSÉ CLAVEROL AND VALENTÍ CLAVEROL

José Claverol Cirici was born on February 15, 1854, in La Seu d'Urgell, Spain. Both his father and an uncle had been doctors in Andorra; notwithstanding that profession, and never forgetting their homeland, they moved their families to La Seu d'Urgell, where they opened a fabric store.

José grew up in prosperous circumstances in La Seu d'Urgell. Orphaned at the age of fourteen, he went to live with an uncle who had emigrated to Chile. It was there that José discovered photography, and the passion remained with him for the rest of his life. When a sister of his in Spain became gravely ill, he returned to La Seu d'Urgell, and while there he met Concepcio Cirici i Mallol. She became his wife.

José and Concepcio had four sons: Josep, Angel, Francesc, and Valentí. Even though the family business was fabric, José set up a photography shop in La Seu d'Urgell. He specialized in studio portraits, popular at that time. He also traveled on horseback or by carriage throughout Catalonia, photographing towns and landscape. These images were later published as postcards by the Bouche et Frère company in Toulouse.

Unfortunately, apart from a collection of postcards, few documents of José Claverol's activity remain. The fragility of the materials (including glass negatives), the many moves, and later the Spanish Civil War all took their toll. While his studio business depended on portraits, complete with painted fictive backgrounds, Claverol adhered to the belief that a good photograph required a natural setting. Nature and authentic urban settings were just as much his subjects as posed individuals and families.

In 1902, with the assistance of an Andorran acquaintance, Claverol persuaded the members of the General Council, the country's parliament, to be photographed—something that had not been done before. It was said that their initial reluctance stemmed from a fear of the camera flash and noise.

José Claverol tried to instill his passion for photography in his oldest son and namesake, but it was the youngest, Valentí, who chose to continue in his father's footsteps. When José died, on November 2, 1921, he left his vocation in good hands.

Valentí Claverol Cirici was born in La Seu d'Urgell on November 24, 1902. Upon his mother's death he moved to Barcelona, where he began working in a fabric store. Seeking to earn extra money, he devoted weekends to photography. He would take pictures principally where he had little or no competition, frequenting the city's polo fields and the aerodrome, among other locations. Soon Eastman Kodak hired him as an office assistant; his talent was finding its route.

In Barcelona, Valentí met Rosa Sesplugas Arrufat, and they married in 1930. Much to his bride's amazement, he chose Andorra for their honeymoon, and there they eventually settled.

Valentí Claverol and his mother, Concepcio, 1902.
(Photograph by José Claverol)

These were not the easiest of times; Claverol had to sell his stock in Kodak to make this new start. He was fulfilling a dream of returning to the home of his ancestors.

He and Rosa settled in Andorra la Vella, where he opened a shop on the main square. They had two children, Dolors and Josep; Josep carries on the family connection to photography, as the importer of Kodak products in Andorra. When his father turned seventy, Josep helped him reestablish his ties with Eastman Kodak: he bought him shares in the company as a birthday present.

The archive created by Valentí Claverol is indispensable to understanding the development of Andorra over much of the twentieth century. Between 1930 and 1970 he captured memorable moments in the country's history, official and less so. Through these photographs and his postcards, he made Andorra known in the world.

VALENTÍ CLAVEROL IN ANDORRA

Valentí Claverol, whose forebears had once lived in Andorra, arrived there from Barcelona in 1930 already trained as a photographer. He had learned the trade from his father, José. Valentí opened one of the first shops in Andorra, where besides photographic materials (he was faithful to Kodak since the 1920s), he sold souvenirs as well as his own postcards, and made photographs to order. For his own work, he took inspiration from the natural and man-made environment of Andorra.

Valentí and his father were the pioneer photographers of the country. They performed the standard tasks of village photographers—producing family and individual portraits, and other pictures made to order—and tried to capture the feeling of the country and disseminate it through their postcards. They built a photographic archive of Andorra, not only matter-of-factly recording events, personalities, and settings, but also rendering the spirit of the country beyond, and through, specific faces and places. Whatever the financial or artistic motives inspiring it, their production is singular, documenting as it does Andorran life from the early part of the century to the more recent past.

There is, certainly, other photographic evidence of Andorra and its history; pictures survive from the nineteenth century, tourists have taken their own snapshots, and travel magazines have sent their own photographers. But Valentí Claverol was the only photographer to have assembled a body of work showing everyday life in twentieth-century Andorra; he was a notary, chronicling transition in this ancient country, and an ethnographer, collecting images of the people, their customs, the surroundings that shape them and that they shape.

For decades Valentí Claverol's shop stood on the main—and only—square of Andorra la Vella, an ideal location to observe life in the capital. All important official events took place on that square: here the Spanish prince bishop and the French head of state arrived on formal visits; here French and Spanish military police forces marched, sent to keep order and protect the country in times of crisis; here Andorrans assembled for meetings, religious processions, and celebrations.

Valentí between his parents,
and flanked by two of his brothers, 1910.
(Photograph by José Claverol)

The four Claverol children,
Josep, Angel, Francesc, and Valentí, 1905.

From this vantage point, and in his travels to the other five parishes of Andorra and the countryside, Claverol produced his unique photographic record. He documented, and thus preserved, the country's opening itself to the rest of the world. Roads to the outside were built, tourists and tradesmen arrived, hotels were erected, shops and businesses opened and expanded; the medieval principality became a tax-free commercial market. The pace of life accelerated, and Andorrans prospered. While it coincided with this acceleration, and with the urbanization of the country, Claverol's documentation also captured an Andorra that is lost to us today. And as the country and its people prospered, his monopoly as a chronicler came to an end: the Instamatic was now an affordable if not ubiquitous item; no longer was Valentí Claverol the only man with a camera.

Valentí Claverol, who died on January 13, 2000, was a witness to the twentieth century. The record of what he saw is a remarkable and ongoing legacy for Andorrans and foreigners alike. As Andorra enters a new century, of undoubtedly more and faster change, his archive is an irreplaceable treasure.

The principality of Andorra honored Valentí Claverol for his work, and he was recognized by UNESCO with the Picasso Medal for his contribution to the cultural heritage of Andorra. In 1975, Kodak Pathé (France) honored him for fifty years of loyal service to Eastman Kodak. Perhaps the greatest honor, however, is this: Andorrans who wish to see images of their ancestors and their country as it was in the past, who are curious about what the village of their birth once looked like, who want to be reminded of landscape and customs that have altered, perhaps even disappeared, will be satisfied by viewing Claverol's archive. And not only will they be informed, they will be heartened as well.

Valentí's wife, Rosa, and her niece Conxita gathering the
grandalla, the official flower of Andorra.

A VISIT TO ANDORRA

KARL KATZ

The name of Andorra was somewhat familiar to most of the people my wife and I queried before making a trip to the principality—a snippet of a country founded in the thirteenth century—a slice of granite and shale, a haven for shoppers, although people also mentioned hikes and birds. We did some reading, of course, but when we went there last summer to see the Valentí Claverol Archives, we didn't know very much more than our friends.

Liz and I were thus prepared for almost anything except the initial dismay that overwhelmed us. At the end of a leisurely and lovely drive from Barcelona, via medieval Gerona, we found ourselves on the main thoroughfare of Andorra la Vella, the country's capital and principal parish, at the bottom of a winding canyon of stores, jostled by shoppers, honked at by other drivers, utterly disoriented. Almost four hundred outlets, from nearly every major manufacturer in the world, can be found in Andorra la Vella (the old), we were told later; the shoppers seemed legion.

These day-trippers, serious consumers from Spain and France, arrive in empty cars and leave fully loaded. They make up most but not all of Andorra's visitors. Others come for the pleasure of the low-lying Pyrenees Mountains that surround it: bird-watchers, hikers, campers.

We met the Claverols, Josep and his son David, the next day, and they led us into the other life of Andorra, its cobblestone streets, its tidy squares, its stately mini parliament building, the historical sites. This walking tour, which wound in and out of the shopping streets—it takes only a few steps to enter or leave this frantic century in the capital—was followed by a short car ride to a neighboring parish, where we found ourselves in the midst of even tidier squares, sprawling cafés, and small hotels. Flowers were everywhere, in sidewalk containers, in window boxes, and in hanging planters that swung in the breeze.

Another ten minutes' ascent with the Claverols into the Pyrenees brought us into the countryside and another small parish, a Lilliputian village in fact, which relies on many small streams to water its animals. The air here was filled with butterflies and birds, and sounds that traveled quite a distance. Scattered about were little plots of tobacco. The Claverols own a house here, and in season, Mrs. Claverol goes with her extraordinary ninety-year-old friend Margarit to gather mushrooms farther up in the mountains.

The last stop of the day, a visit to the Valentí Claverol Archives in Andorra la Vella, transported us into the realm of Andorra's historical, social, and architectural past. We found ourselves wandering through images of people and places we knew were gone forever.

We remembered, as we studied those marvelous photographs, that the next day we would be leaving Andorra, and contemplated the hordes of shoppers once again descending on it. We remembered as well the construction sites we had seen throughout the day, spreading over both sides of the Pyrenees. More people, more building would doubtlessly come over the years, but this archive would not—could not—be crowded out, and for that we were very glad.

THE SPANISH PHOTOGRAPHS

The Claverol family lived for several years in the Spanish town of La Seu d'Urgell. This enabled José Claverol to travel extensively throughout Catalonia, on horseback and by carriage, photographing village life and landscape at the end of the nineteenth century. Many of these images were later published and sold as popular postcards, now highly sought after by collectors.

Valentí Claverol left La Seu d'Urgell after his mother died, and moved to Barcelona, photographing the city and its environs in his spare time to earn extra income. His pictures, taken in the twenties and early thirties, capture a changing Spain, very different from the place and the way of life that his father had recorded earlier in the century.

During this period, Valentí also took delightful pictures of friends and relations on carefree country outings, a few examples of which are included here.

This selection of Spanish photographs by Valentí Claverol is being published for the first time.

OVERLEAF: The co-prince of Andorra, bishop of
Urgell (wearing robes) awaiting the visit of a member
of the Spanish royal family in La Seu d'Urgell,
c. 1895. (Photograph by José Claverol)

ABOVE: A village in Catalonia, 1925.

OPPOSITE: The village of Livia, 1924.

ABOVE: The hospital of Santa Creu, Barcelona, 1924.

OPPOSITE: Maritime club, port of Barcelona, 1924.

ABOVE: Cloister of Sant Cugat, Catalonia, 1925.

OPPOSITE: Procession of the Holy Christ of Montserrat, 1927.

President Francesc Macia (with white flower in lapel),
Barcelona, c. 1930.

TOP: The funeral of Francesc Macia, Barcelona, 1933.

BOTTOM: The Andorran delegation to the funeral, 1933.

ABOVE: An excursion to Montmelo, Catalonia, 1925.

OPPOSITE: An excursion to Llorens de Munt, Catalonia, 1924.

ABOVE: A picnic at La Seu d'Urgell, 1924.

OPPOSITE: On the road to Vallvidredra, 1924.

Published on the occasion of *Andorran Memories*, a retrospective exhibition of photographs by
Valentí Claverol, organized by The Spanish Institute in New York.

First Edition

ISBN 188558616-7

Library of Congress Catalogue Card Number 00 130185

"Claverol," "V. Claverol," and "Valentí Claverol" are all trademarks of
Josep Claverol Ltd., a United Kingdom limited-liability company.

This book was prepared and produced by Constance Sullivan
Designed by Katy Homans

Duotone separations by Robert J. Hennessey
Printed and bound by L.E.G.O., Vicenza, Italy

Printed in Italy

Illustrations
PAGE 1: Map of Andorra surrounded by France and Spain, 1790. Private collection.

PAGE 2: The main street of the village of Canillo, 1932.
The houses have electricity but no running water.

GATEFOLD: Map of Andorra surrounded by France and Spain, 1789. Private Collection.